Agnes in the sky

AGNES IN THE SKY

DI BRANDT

TURNSTONE PRESS

Turnstone Press
607-100 Arthur Street
Winnipeg, Manitoba
Canada   R3B 1H3

Turnstone Press gratefully acknowledges the assistance of the Manitoba Arts Council and the Canada Council.

Cover illustration: *Figures with Animals and Clouds by a Farm* (1986) by Ann Smith, collage and mixed media, 30½" x 20¼".

Cover design: Terry Gallagher.

This book was printed and bound in Canada by Kromar Printing Limited.

Canadian Cataloguing in Publication Data

Brandt, Diana

Agnes in the sky

Poems.
ISBN 0-88801-150-4

I. Title.

PS8553.R2953A73 1990   C811/.54   C90-097124-X
PR9199.3.B726A73 1990

Some of these poems have appeared previously in
Arc, *Border Crossings*, *Healing Voices*, *The Mennonite
Mirror*, *The New Quarterly*, *Prairie Fire*
and *Language in Her Eye* and have been aired
on CBC's "Speaking Volumes."

With thanks to Joan Turner, Richard Harrison,
Heidi Harms, Pat Sanders, Wayne Tefs, Paula Kelly,
Marilyn Morton, and Ann Smith.

for Joan
who made this story possible

& for Richard
who listened with such care

finding out what happens after
you fall off the edge, continuing.

Daphne Marlatt, *Our Lives*

the floor sags
like a ship floundering;

we know no rule
of procedure,

we are voyagers, discoverers
of the not-known,

the unrecorded;
we have no map;

possibly we will reach haven,
heaven.

H.D., *The Walls Do Not Fall*

contents

the banquet in your mind

so many different kinds of love

if i told even a sliver of what i know
who would listen

prairie love song

the banquet in your mind

so this is the world & here i am
after all in the middle of it one of
the many broken hearted so far
across the centuries away from
home living each day for what it
may bring without sorrow or pity
for the lost kingdom face to the wind
this time mother please don't take
away my pain let's just say it is
mine & this is the world & here i am
in it hidden amazed among the trees
one of the many lost & found if you
can believe it across all this space
& i think i can say this from so far
away that i love you i love you

already there is no going back
the trees curl around your
feet the air is full of messages
you miss the father in your
bones the rain falls warm
on your cheek you stand alone
at the world's edge your soul
is worth diamonds your feet
are heavy with the weight
of it which way you whisper
mother please

the dead father
(after Barthelme)

killing him that was the easy part
cutting off his legs hands arms neck
dismembering his armoured chest
dismantling the intricate cogwheels
of his brain digging through iron
to the bruised purple swollen heart
throwing the remains bits & pieces
to the mob their tongues hanging
out scattering crown jewels to the
dogs getting rid of the dead man that
was the easy part digging uneasily
through rubble to the fresh dirt
growing new fingers to rummage
in the earth nurture new seedlings
to life resist despair dreaming last
night of our bodies hands stroking
each other with such tenderness
such tenderness staying alive in
the broken world this lost planet
finding in all the uneasiness after
the carnage so far past believing
a new start

the man in the pulpit quotes Jesus
& Shakespeare to prove the world
is still round a perfect circle in
God's eye in spite of acid rain & the
hole above Antarctica ripping the sky
apart he believes the world is made
of words let me not the words are
magic to the marriage of true minds
if he pulls enough magenta coloured
scarves from his coatsleeves we
will believe the hole in our minds
will disappear & the dead lakes rise
up & dance with the trees admit
impediments while this white bride
kisses this black prince & all around
us there is the faint rustling of leaves

the way the body disappears into thin
wafers your hands on my flesh black
lines on a page the gardens of Adonis
were broken clay pots once set on old
rooftops & filled with myrrh the air
was laden with the sound of women
weeping their tears became jewels
in their chests the way we replace
old blood with new wine the thinning
of metaphor the way we talked about
forever choosing our brand the tart
flavour of charcoal in the mouth the way
the body disappears

3 poems for Agnes

1

you count the ten ways of saving
Agnes you recite them to yourself
in the night bake a chocolate cake
call the priest find her sister not
the one in River Heights the younger
one you think somewhere in St.
Vital with crutches walking the
dog chatting across the verandah
the weather the mosquitoes her
dead mother her heart listening
to the ragged story one more round
spiralling toward the black hole
in the ground ignoring the paint man
& the cabbie & the beer your arm
around her just this once eye to eye
without wincing hold your breath
Christmas turkey apple pie careening
down Jessie giddily the old street
car named Desire *oh Blanche Blanche*

2

& then you remember the broken
engagement the crystal laid out
on the mahogany table the candles
the lace you remember the ticket
office at the train station & the
soldiers back from the war how
he held her among the crowd his
arm proud his breath on her cheek
our Agnes panting her love on Main
Street face flushed & no priest
how she waited all those months
& years after Christmas with her
prayers & her beads & how she
finally heard from her sister about
the retarded child in California
growing up American God's punishment
for an afternoon's sin on the beach
though he still loved her Agnes &
not the other *it could have been you*
the way he let her tell everyone in
Winnipeg graciously it was her wish
oh her endless forgiving & her spirits
& her priest & no one to care about
the story now Agnes not even you

3

& suddenly you want desperately
to believe in her angels & her
saints their satin robes shining
somewhere above Jupiter you want
her to have found a place in some
holy choir the Virgin blessing heaven
with her tears you want for Agnes
in the sky some holy black prince
caressing her broken spirit bones
into light all the desperate nights
on earth forgotten you find yourself
standing on the corner in front of
her house at dusk clasping your hands
strange you should miss her so when
you've agreed with the rest she's
much better off dead & the new
neighbours so much younger & lively
Agnes in the sky with diamonds

the watcher

watching her forget & remember
& forget that was the hardest
part the way she ran silverquick
through the trees barefoot afraid
never never once looking back
all those years wandering so
carelessly through ditches never
losing the brightness & waiting
that long winter's day after the
crash for the evening light Goldne
Abend Sonne the flash of it breaking
in her eyes *wie bist du so schön*

at Basil's

Menno's sons meet every Wednesday
evening at Basil's for beer they
pretend they've gone worldly eat
chicken fingers with honey dip
burn each other's cigarettes but
the room is made of mirrors & if
you look past their jokes & their
bland faces you can see the backs
of their heads through the smoke
beginning to crack open & Menno's
guts spilling out Jake wears his
baseball cap everywhere even to bed
so he won't have to think about the
split in his skull getting wider each
year his mother worries about him
Pete figured out long ago how to
make the room dance he doesn't mind
the numbness in his chest after the
third or so it reminds him strangely
of home though he will cry someday
Pete will for another chance & where
will Menno's promises be then & where
was God when all these young men
felt their souls crumble to dust &
where is he now when all i can see
in the mirror is the vines & tendrils
of something wild growing in their
brains & where's my long lost brother
Mike who might have inherited the
earth with me Menno where's Mike

no footing here no solid
ground flailing about in
water feet can't touch
bottom no feet drifting
in air help no breathe no
air the ground shifting
the sluck sluck of quick
sand mother *help me*
please there is no one
try to be rational build
a bridge out of wood pieces
floating by lay them one
by one beside each other
float sink flail about gulp
for air how did you get
here the dead smell close
air green warm feeling of
swamp muck legs & arms
green with swamp lace
naked flesh crying for
its old skin *please* letting
it wash over you warm
& green & alive

i'm finding myself again in the healed heart
(for Joan Turner   with love)

& suddenly   i'm little again   so little   i daren't
breathe or make a sound   i'm staring through crib bars
at a blank wall   the room is big & far away   the
world is full of wonder   if i move or make a sound it
will happen again   do what he says a voice whispers
in my ear   do what he says   or he will kill you   i'm
locked   frozen with fear   i'm too little to understand
fear   my whole being trembles with shock   what is
happening   do what he says the voice whispers   &
i'll watch out for you   i'll watch   don't make a sound
remember this for your life   remember   & suddenly
you're here in the room with me   i'm a grown
woman   i'm so little   lying on this table huddled in
my crib   why don't you make some sounds   you say
your strong soft hands stroking my back   i'm frozen
with fear   my whole being trembles with shock
now that you're grown up & can break the rules   you
say again   your hands stroking my back   make some
sounds   i'm scared   i've waited all my life for this
moment   & yes   i let it come up   a huge ancient
cry   a wail from somewhere deep inside me   deeper
than my bones   deeper than my womb   a cry of
children left alone in the night   the cry of women
with torn bellies screaming pain   the cry of trees
ripped from the earth in huge furrows   a cry of oceans
reeling with blood   i cry my small loneliness my
betrayal my fear   i cry all my years of numbness &

confusion   i cry my father's anger   his knowledge
his cruel hands   i cry my mother's silence   her fear
i cry the joy of the earth's my own wanting   it washes
over me in a great wave   it'll break my bones washing
over me i think   it'll break the world smash the crib
bars shatter the table   but i'm after all only a baby
my grown woman's pain comes out a small baby's cry
so little   the cry spills out of me like rain like laughter
onto the table into the room   & suddenly i'm
laughing   my baby's body shakes with laughing   you
bastard   i laugh i gurgle i crow   you thought you
could break me possess me own me   you thought you
could make me live in fear   on *nothing*   past your
grave   past your dying   forever   you didn't know
someday i'd get free   & i'm smiling   smiling full of
light   & over my shoulder i see her   the watcher
her beautiful calm face   her radiance   her deep
eyes   & suddenly i see that she is me   & the
moment i see this   the moment i know myself   she
is gone   & i feel an opening in my chest   i'm
finding myself again in the healed heart   & my
father's spirit is beside me blessing me with his tears
my father who cried with such anguish when he knew
what he'd done   & he didn't know even then after
death my father he didn't know such an outrage such a
great wounding could be undone   & he's glad   the
split years roll away   my father is no more   the hole
in my heart closes gently   my mother does not move
the trees outside the window shiver their ancient

14

secrets   you cradle me in your arms   tenderly   you
cover my nakedness with the cool scented sheet   you
touch my cheek   hold me miracle fairy godmother my
sweet   grown woman little child   the room is so big
& far away   the world is full of wonder

stepping onto dry ground the huge
relief of it the earth firm under
your feet the old mother smell
of roots grass flowers leaves
filling your lungs the feel of her
soft arm on your neck her hands
stroking your body with such
tenderness knowing yourself in
a new place the trees so green
this summer so green the world
newly made & eighteen again
with washed eyes dancing all
alone the scent on the breeze of
the sweet tufted truffula trees

you prepare a banquet in your mind
for your mother & the man who shared
your grief in the night & the woman
who saved your life & your beautiful
daughters you gather wildflowers to
put at their places fireweed foxtail
goldenrod you collect acorns you paint
the table you hang ribbons from the
trees you order sweet nectar you leave
a place for the stranger you write to
your sister you inscribe the invitations
in green ink festooned with garlands
you scatter the ground with ash seeds
you imagine a feast you prepare a
banquet in your mind for your mother

the day i met you something in me fell
away some old voice the body's tonal
grieving your voice your hands your
eyes opened a new place in my scarred
heart until then i had thought of you
only in dreams a song to measure the
world's failings by i believed though
i didn't want to the old guys who said
desire is always for what you can't
get i coloured my atmosphere like others
with regret thinking with the rest that
the offspring of poverty is beautiful
a desperate mothering the only reprieve
from war i believed in the great battle
cry of love the hunting down the grand
chord of opposites crashing together
the day i met you something in me fell
away some old voice the body's tonal
grieving remembering an earlier time
in the light we're walking in light the
air is clear & there's singing we're
holding each other gently walking in
light

you come bearing gifts green apples
glistening in a red bowl you have
waited all your life for this moment
tended your small tree carefully
weathered high winds listened to
the world's pain each delicate
exquisite hurt you have wept &
fasted & prayed you have waited
in the garden beside the rose bushes
at night you have sculpted this
container out of earth with your
bare hands you have looked for your
mother you walk through the green
fields slowly your heart is singing
the sun glitters on your back

so many different kinds of love

one thing poking around in the garden
behind bushes & under strawberry
leaves because that's where you found
your mother one summer picking beans
humming sweet Jesus looking for juice
stains but also feathers & nests in the
sun the black earth hot clodded under
your feet quite another making your way
back to it through flames the anger of
the Lord searing your left arm like a
scar your desire fierce & dull & throbbing
a hump on your back that won't go away
no matter how hard how hard you pray
another thing clawing your way back to
fruit & vegetables the *blessed* digging
all night & then praying for rain the
neighbours staring not remembering the
spring its underground bubbling its red
earthed its blue oracled babbling

small earth trilogy
(for H.D.)

1

coming to greet you in the corridor
the lost golden boys with their wounds
the whiff of an old choir-song your
mother & her sisters dancing round
the golden calf *drede Heljedag* not
caring a fig about Moses & his wrath
yes & with Grandma in cahoots you
& your sisters posed as Muses for the
camera on the beach Jesus listening
to country music with his beard shaved
off Mary mother Mary when will my
true lord come i'm lost i'm oh so lonely
languishing in shade dreaming empty
hieroglyphs on empty walls Helen
shimmering phantom-like Egyptian
the sea-enchanted the gold-burning
sands

2

finding another beside me in the dying
world unexpectedly proffering love i ask
Jesus i ask Isis give us this day a future
to hold in our hands a pearl a bead a comb
a cup a bowl glinting half hidden in the
sand Aganetha Justina Maria hiding your
laughter in the barn give me more give me
more than stones i want red raspberries
& wild roses blooming in the snow the
shoes of dancing princesses spilling the
inkwell & the Sen Sen & the Word the cow
kicking over the milking stool all the cats
saved Mary Nettie Sarah Leina Jessie &
Annie *the holy ghost* shaking your red gold
brown hair perfumed against the sun your
secret fire your flaming desire

3

chant the words slowly on your tongue
trace the Egyptian lines on your face
once again with your hand now is the
time of grace now is the time of harvest
squeeze the purple fruit rudely into your
mouth dribble it down your chin all that
must die can now be reborn Rosie Rosie
Ring arounda Rosie *aurora borealis* every
ransomed daughter a jewelled princess
yo! let the rivers flow let the prairie
grass grow let the wild rice sow its old
magic in the wind let the God shaped
papyrus shaped hole in our hearts disappear
the great styrofoam wound in the sky
weeping be healed

fathers never leave you

(for Richard Harrison)

fathers never leave you he said
& i cried standing under the elm
tree at dusk smelling the leaves
thinking of fathers how they leave
you & leave you Henry & Peter &
Jacob screaming with anger in the
belly & not a sound in your throat
how they loved their bearded sacrifice
& their judgements & their flames
circumscribing the world with a
heavy hand cutting down trees in a
northern bush camp to defend their
Word breaking the land & the horses
& the children into stupid submission
how you are left trembling still alone
in the night by their crippled sons
& how you will spend your whole life
& your daughters crying for enough
love *they never leave you* he said &
he meant it as something true in the
broken world & i heard it that way as
a promise breaking the heart's silence
like a song & a cry & a possibility of
coming back across the dark earth &
a healing

so many different kinds of love

(for Dennis Cooley)

so many different kinds of love & war Jack
& you adept at so many & me willing like you
to lay my body down try my luck sneaking
around in bushes at night brandishing weapons
so many different kinds piecing it together
from kibbles & bits what we won't settle for
in a ditch chance encounter of a lifetime huh
never sure if it's kissing we want or a fist
is it a bloody game Jack or is this real life
crying for knife wounds in the belly & hugs
in the chest & me like you willing to lay my
body down

since we cannot meet on father ground
our father's land as sister & brother ever
let's imagine a new place between us
slightly suspended in air but yet touching
earth an old tree house full of weather
or an ark its ancient hull gleaming
remembering the rains let's gather our
belongings & our children & meet at the
river this will be a new country love &
crossing the field to greet you i will lay
my old weapons down & wait if you are
there with me under the harvest moon
we will look in each other's eyes without
speaking our hands will shake & the great
wooden door will begin creaking open at
last since we cannot meet

this is the ceremony of innocence
wherein the white knight lost in
thought after his latest doubtful
move against or for his sad queen
steps off the checkered path & wanders
bemused into the woods where he
meets a black sheep who is similarly
lost after straying from her family
flock & they exchange greetings &
a gift he withdraws the poison from
her skin she washes his fatal lance
with her wool coming together to a
windswept hill they look up at the sky
her garment begins to shine more radiant
than the snow his armour turns to gold
behind them the ghosts of their wounded
mothers rise out of the leaf lined caves
& begin to sing & she becomes a bride
& he becomes a shepherd king

(for Heidi)

you take the tears a woman
might cry in middle age after
a lifetime of swallowing them
whole one by one gagging slowly
in the night you let them out
tenderly stroke each sob gently
into life watch them grow around
her profusely like wildflowers
or weeds sometimes they're
like a river in spring swollen
with snow from the hills or
babies without mothers screaming
themselves silently to sleep
sometimes there's such quiet
in the middle of it you think it's
over but before long you understand
that was only the sadness needing
to breathe you take the tears a
woman might cry in a lifetime
over her babies & her lost lovers
& her grief watch them spill richly
& strange to the ground not even
Solomon in his glory was surrounded
with such splendour nor are lilies
arrayed in garments such as these

middle age

you grow new skin mercifully
to house the flaming flesh listen
at night to death growing darkly
in your bones you throw away
extravagantly your purple fears
the green shadows on the walls
you give your grandmother's black
flowered shawl to a stranger you
walk around the unspeakableness
that was you gingerly the way
earthquake survivors point at
wrecked houses shaking their heads
you scatter the old skin like ashes
crushed stone among iris when
strangers speak you look at them
curiously with turquoise lidded
eyes your hand reaching out to the
world as it rises to meet you is
empty

you find yourself alone in a room
with your mother at last you can
ask her anything & she will tell
you she turns her head toward you
graciously & reaches out her arm
her hand when it touches you is
not clutching neither is it a fist
the Virgin above her head reminds
you gently there is only one chance
whatever you ask in this blue dusk
will be granted but only once your
heart cries out its huge ancient cry
there is never enough love it isn't
a matter of asking you think of your
own daughters & their love tests how
you've failed spectacularly each one
if mothers were angels or stone you
could wrestle them for it *bless me
or i will not let you go* if you could
go back in the dark to that first place
where you & your mother were alone
what do you want from her in this
last hour or is it something you
should give you remember the first
the loneliest betrayal her arm around
you just this once shielding you from
your father's hands *No!* this is where
it stops knowing she couldn't & why

if she could have embroidered the world
in her colours what would they have been
if we had met in a garden as sisters
or strangers our eyes meeting briefly
across roses what might we have said
before the wind blew the leaves back
our fingers touching lightly reaching
for stems

hold on to your smallness little one
hold on to your grief feeling so like
a hot knife wound in the chest carry
it with you hug it fiercely to your
breast feed it bitter herbs & vinegar
watch it grow teeth don't let it out
until it's strong enough to breathe
dragonfire till it breaks from your
hands like thunder scorches the air
spits stones scars the earth then
hide yourself little one hide in the
smoke bite your tongue seal your lips
against pity & wonder walk through
the flames you have made without
flinching let it singe your hair a little
what do you care if you can learn
to dance on live coals you will live
forever your smallness will become
a golden bowl spilling sapphires
& then you can scatter your dazzling
grief on the lawn like flowers freshly
cut in the sun

wedding poem for Phyllis, 1989

so much easier to talk about forever
when you're nineteen & still believe
in roses & the world is your father's
house you think you will escape by
staying up all night dancing with
younger men & the answer to your
mother's crease lined face & shabby
linen & faded hair is love transforming
everything to gold so much easier
to slide into household dust & diapers
& car rust with your nose buried in
a bouquet & your eyelids delicately
shaded yet you remember nothing
from those years that wasn't hard work
including the stories we told over
coffee the way we twisted ourselves
mornings around full & empty lives
inventing our escape finding yourself
in a garden once more with your children
carrying roses you turn the word love
over curiously on your tongue this time
not a running away or a leaping but
a promise made wide eyed in daylight
with the knowledge of time & loss &
hurt in your hands a stretching toward
the horizon tenderly of darling & forever

you stand under the green tree
at dusk smelling the leaves
you look at the transparent
sky you hold out your arms
you are an old woman without
tears your breasts do not
remember children in the palm
of your hand the earth feels
like granite you whisper the
names of the beloved each
worn out name you scatter the
knotted syllables to the air
tenderly your mouth opens &
closes the world's wound soft
like the velvet of this green
edged leaf

if i told even a sliver of what i know
who would listen

nonresistance, or love Mennonite style
(for L. & the others)

turn the other cheek when your brother
hits you & your best friend tells fibs
about you & the teacher punishes you
unfairly if someone steals your shirt
give him your coat to boot this will
heap coals of fire on his head & let him
know how greatly superior you are
while he & his cronies dicker & bargain
their way to hell you can hold your
head up that is down humbly knowing
you're bound for the better place where
it gets tricky is when your grandfather
tickles you too hard or your cousins
want to play doctor & your uncle kisses
you too long on the lips & part of you
wants it & the other part knows it's
wrong & you want to run away but you
can't because he's a man like your father
& the secret place inside you feels itchy
& hot & you wonder if this is what hell
feels like & you remember the look on
your mother's face when she makes
herself obey your dad & meanwhile her
body is shouting *No! No!* & he doesn't
even notice & you wish you could stop
being angry all the time but you can't
because God is watching & he sees

everything there isn't any place to let
it out & you understand about love the
lavish sacrifice in it how it will stretch
your woman's belly & heap fire on your
head you understand how love is like
a knife & a daughter is not a son & the
only way you will be saved is by
submitting quietly in your grandfather's
house your flesh smouldering in the
darkened room as you love your enemy
deeply unwillingly & full of shame

this is how wounded people
love each other from far away
fielding the distance between
them with words listening
to the hum of telephone wires
emptying envelopes waiting
between sounds for a slight
catch in the voice a tremor in
the breath reaching between
lines for the hurt behind the
words instead of lies they
send each other poems circling
elegantly around old wounds
their bodies when they touch
are only names their faces
on the page are well arranged

if i told even a sliver of what i know
who would listen if i cracked open
the chestnut coloured beads around
my neck if i danced all night to the
drumming blood & collapsed at your
feet at daybreak if i clutched your
feet as you were leaving if i sang
the sweet siren song of the sea if
i showed the stigmata on my hands
& feet if as they were turning to go
i caught one's eyes over her shoulder
winningly *yes* she might say turning
yes if i rolled everything up into a
ball compressed thunder to a smile
if i told even a sliver of what i know
haltingly who would listen

scapegoat

someone had to die because that's
what the story was someone had
to die sometimes it was enough
if you went crazy for a while or
cut off your hand accidentally with
a chainsaw or something terrible
happened like someone's children
getting killed in a housefire or a
fatal car accident *an act of God*
people would say wisely nodding
their heads it wasn't enough that
one time on the hill one man's death
taking the place of all it had to be
repeated in every generation every
family someone had to die pull all
his hair out run off become a thief
go bad usually the sensitive angry
one the stray out of the ninety nine
nothing like a black sheep to make
a yellowish flock feel white ah but
the best deaths were the innocents
the babies the daughters with the
golden hair & most of all mothers
sweet white ghost mothers cheerfully
sacrificing themselves to the world
denying themselves into goodness
so the rest of the black sinful clan
could be saved by their dying

because you wanted too much
too soon because you weren't
my father because you looked
at me in the doorway like he
did because you couldn't give
me what he didn't because it
was less painful to repeat than
to remember because you hated
women when you loved them
because i wasn't your mother
because i didn't die like she did
because i didn't listen & i wasn't
crazy when i went black in
September because you couldn't
save me i couldn't save you
because i started crying & then
i couldn't stop because of the hole
inside me because i loved you
crookedly because you weren't
my father

mother feeling

the time my mother locked
herself in the bathroom to cry
because she wasn't dead & the
others were the time i needed
her so much & she wasn't there
& the time she was the times
i wanted to die & the time i
tried *i do it so it feels like hell
i do it so it feels real* the time
i went numb over the mother
feeling & the time it made me
alive the times i've loved the
mother in me like a queen & the
time i saw cruelty in her face
the time you held me like a
mother the time i held myself
the times i've screamed at the
motherless world the times
i've received her that time i
knew i was made of earth that
time i knew she loved me

i hate love

it just hurts like hell &
where does it ever get you
watching the heart open
against wishing against
the old wound's wisdom
again again the prairies
folding around your desire
like postage stamps licked
& sent the air full of
messages contrary to logic
contrary to the space that
exists between us that's
what you said you're too
far away & me not remembering
the geography the days of
the week not remembering
distances only the light
falling slanted & radiant
around you in the kitchen
your arms strong & tender
in spite of the words said
& not said in an afternoon
where does it ever get you

true confession

i wanted the story to be true
i wanted everything to be my
fault the mistakes the violence
at the heart of it i wanted to
swallow the dark world hug it
sweatingly to my belly seven
days seven nights to save their
faith their sweet diamond city
howling smashing against the
gate at night gnashing my teeth
i wanted it all to be my fault
obediently yes rather than
meet them on the high road my
father's red eyed hounds her
curved knives their stony silence
around my desire the blank stare

children like us

the exiled the disinherited
the ones with broken knees
children like us whose skin
is not their own whose flesh
remembers the generations
& their tears who are filled
with the world's longing &
call it love who bruise too
easily like fresh fruit the
gifted the innocent the broken
hearted who hear voices in
the trees who've seen the sky
become transparent at sunset
& know eternity in their bones
the beautiful the lost whose
cries keep the earth alive whose
flesh is like grass like flaming
the orphaned the poor in spirit
suffering earth's children

the one who lives underwater
the one who hears what is said
& not said in the room the one
who knows too much & is willing
to pay the one who never cries
the one who hoards the family
stories secretly who feels her
way in the dark the one who has
no right because she was the
gifted favourite child the one who
knows terror before it happens
who tries to hold night together
with her breath if she gives them
what they ask for if she never says
if she makes herself smaller than
what she is they will be saved from
her knowing she thinks incredibly
the rest of the world will be saved

long distance

the way we couldn't name our fear
on the phone that time taking over
our voices throats chests *the wave*
you called it remembering your mother
engulfing you with her pain & you
keeping the fear alive years after
with other women i held completely
in it my body receiving your mother's
pain like a cup full of sorrow & you
far away & invisible your mother
a stranger to me trying to remember
my own fear with other women other
men & knowing only this being held
completely by the feeling fear deep
& close to desire the way i loved my
father after he beat me as the deepest
thing i knew & you said let's hang up
& start over & it worked the mercy
of long distance & middle age thirty
years' confusion disappeared with a
click the way we held ourselves perfectly
in that moment our bodies in our voices
together & alone & full of tenderness
& unafraid

teaching in prison

(for my students at Stony Mountain)

you teach me the dignity of desperate
men how to live with my ear to the ground
hands open & bent or curled around nothing
like babies' fists behind your too old eyes
i see your still kept innocence your young
boy's love the way you look at each other
& at me imagining another place your
bones knowing already the cold old call
of the boneyard the dark sweet smell of
Mother Earth the way you listen to words
not for the meaning but for the sound of
them deep in the throat the way you
remember behind these walls hunger &
cold & sweetgrass & woodsmoke the flick
of a knife in winter the walls of your
grandmother's house

prairie love song

sea song, river song

who was it that held you
in the night rocking from
side to side in your bed
like a sea who kept you
from driving every morning
past the end of the dock
into the red river who
waited for you all the dark
winter calling smiling
who brought you to spring
who was it that carried
you pushed you to dying
second birth who found you
gasping dangling like a
hooked fish who flipped
you back into freshwater
who saved you

the sound of your grief
echoes in the room like
a wildwoman's singing
your ears perk to the rise
& fall of it the heart's
keening somewhere inside
you there is a word for
lost child & wind & star
somewhere inside you are
forests where the lost
women are who might have
been who might have been
holding out their arms
with eyes made of diamonds
& vine leaves in their hair

why my father beat us
(when we were little)

so we would swallow the Punisher
eat him whole so we'd know the
Punisher in our bellies & not his
face so he wouldn't have to beat
us growing up so we would honour
& obey him so we would be good &
even now after all the screaming
I've done all the letting go there
is still the place in my back like
a hole a wall in the house ripped
away if you touch me if you punch
me there by mistake you will see
the Punisher not his face but his
power twisting my features into
fright oh you can't get rid of the
Punisher when you've known him
like that how he loves the big
fight he was too big for us Daddy
too big even for you remembering
the sting of leather on your own
little back & once you've known him
like that as you know Daddy you
can't get rid of him the Punisher
in black

my father's hands

my father's hands could fix anything
from combines to plumbing to the
telephone he never read directions
he just fumbled around with whatever
it was until it worked with his thick
hands my father broke horses broke
prairie into farmland pounded nails
into wood my father's hands could fix
anything even our feet our sore ankles
rubbing them at the end of the day
with rough fingers & alcohol to take
out the ache with his hands my father
grinning built us the world his quick
hands could fix anything there was fire
in them my father's rough hands

so now you know about
the cruelty of flowers
the heartbreak in them
how they can fill a room
with a beloved's absence
proclaim against flesh
their unreasoning sense
you know how long past
wilting the thought in
the brief leaves will last
how the ache in your throat
at the ends of words is
caught & held by such
delicateness the perfume
in the petals proof enough
against the absolute of
distances the cold hard
logic of our separate selves
embarrassed before such
a lavish display of unbidden
wealth i wish this morning
they had not been sent to
disturb my daily categories
my comfortable grief with
such tender stubbornness
such irrefutable grace such
longing over breakfast for
gardens & trees & your arms

& later you think *no*
the real heartbreak
is in the poem the way
you can make the world
dance on a page the
overwhelming eloquence
of words the way an
image placed just so
can make the sky shake
the irresistible Romance
of language the way you
can grab people by the
throat & make them listen
yet you cannot for a
moment resurrect your
father's bones bring back
the lost children save
Ethiopia resist old age
the way you can write
about love & make it sound
convincing & even beautiful
but cannot rewrite the
geography of our hurt the
way you cannot in spite of
rivers & seasons & flowers
reverse the flow into
nothingness the inevitable
daily ritual of loss

on the terrace of the Porta Nigra
(for Stephan & Barbara)

was hätten wir uns sagen sollen Simon
on the terrace of the Porta Nigra in the
sun the lost tourists milling around us
the sun in our eyes before we began
quarrelling away the afternoon what
should we have said & the look of the
girl beside you hurt & smiling the old
buildings in the market behind you
sad like me Brigitta shaking her hair
against the sun her long blonde arms
her beautiful throat the voices of the
women inside her chiming Laura &
Gudrun *die ungehaltene* how i loved
you that golden moment Desdemona
sitting there so easily on the Porta
Nigra laughing at the sun why not to
Frankfurt you said why not to Paris
all of us dreaming what might have
been on the Porta Nigra before Wilfried
with his God talk his *moralisches*
Leben needing to seize the moment
& make it his own & you Simon wanting
so much like me to save the afternoon
between us stretch out the moment
of leaving the completeness of it ah
golden Brigitta ah Simon your hair
the colour of ripe wheat your hands

filled with music your lost longing
what should we have said before it all
slipped away from us on the terrace
of the Porta Nigra the tourists milling
around us the sun hot in our eyes

phone lover

soooo phone lover phantom lover
do you really exist do you have
skin do you have lips teeth are
you more than air did i invent
you phone lover whispering sweet
things in my ear are you really
there at night when my bed feels
empty though it's narrow & soft
do you have arms waiting for me
somewhere inside this hard
plastic cradling my cheek phone
lover you're so close i can feel
your breath almost taste your
skin

prairie hymn

what i want is the shape of the story of the blood
jolting seasonally to & from the heart underneath
the small gestures of our hands the words spoken
& unspoken between us i want the huge narrative
of the river the curved cry of the land i want the
straight blowing of birch leaves in strong wind
the whistling of prairie grass your lit face in the
distance coming to meet me your arms hot like
August prairie sky all around me

a brave leaping in air toward
the nothing of sky imagining
a haven heaven that isn't there
flinging ourselves across oceans
through unimaginable terrors
to meet for an hour under glass
the flickering light of this blue
dome planes crashing overhead
let me look at you savour the
cerveza in my mouth your eyes
the green tree behind you this
fallen leaf invisible arms that
have held you flying dizzily
through the universe kept you
alive this fear we have of
ecstasy earth's embrace this
fear we have of flying coming
home

nausea

we must believe it can happen we must believe
what the eye sees & the heart knows trembling
we must believe in the slow dying of the earth
the accumulation of toxic wastes plastic pop can
rings strangling sea birds poisoning fish we must
believe in the slow dying of the river where you
sat last summer watching muskrats across the
small channel digging their house of mud under
the fireweed while you searched for the precise
word to describe the shade of sky above the foot
bridge pale lemon transparent lemon orange framing
the bright purple weeds we must believe in the
fierceness of the fear that attacks us at night like
hunger like rage it is not the Earth that betrays us
just as the meaning of hunger is not in the shortage
of food & it is not our rage that will kill us but
the absence of rage walking the footpath along the
boulevard you remember the nausea you once felt
at not being a tree you remember the grove of goddesses
murky shadows dancing & holding out their hands
you understand in the glowing dusk how you are
utterly alone how you are small in the huge universe
you lift up your eyes from the gravel path with its
precise strewn pebbles to the green trees we must
believe it is possible the blood whispers urgently
to go on living we must believe in the trees

prairie love song

think of me when you think of me
as prairie grass deep rooted long
armed reaching through dark soil
through the long summer searching
for underground rain while the sky
shimmers with dust along the horizon
singeing the green earth brown &
the spectacular throated meadow
larks have trouble with their singing
think of me as parched think of me
as flaming my white limbs rooting
in the dark earth deep & cool & full
of longing

piecing together the alphabet
of desire under this evening
lamp's glow the cobblestone
sidewalks in Trier illuminated
manuscripts the old world
reeling about you Helen's fierce
battle with the Word her body's
shattering into speech all over
the night sky tonight i think of
you with hunger fierce & naked
like a child's cry the first &
oldest grammar torn from our
lips & made eloquent through
the years' twisting until we're
stretched thin like parchment
transparent if we're lucky &
occasionally luminous